BRAINS, BRAINS, BRAINS,

and Other HORRIFYING BREAKFASTS

Ali Vega

Lerner Publications ◆ Minneapolis

Lerner Publications Company
A division of Lerner Publishing Group, Inc.
241 First Avenue North
Minneapolis, MN 55401 USA

For reading levels and more information, look up this title at www.lernerbooks.com.

Main body text set in Tw Cen MT Std.
Typeface provided by Monotype.

Library of Congress Cataloging-in-Publication Data

Names: Vega, Ali, author.
Title: Brains, brains, and other horrifying breakfasts / by Ali Vega.
Description: Minneapolis : Lerner Publications, [2017] | Series: Little kitchen of horrors | Audience: Ages 7-11. | Audience: Grades 4 to 6. | Includes bibliographical references and index.
Identifiers: LCCN 2016019124 (print) | LCCN 2016020252 (ebook) | ISBN 9781512425789 (lb : alk. paper) | ISBN 9781512428049 (eb pdf)
Subjects: LCSH: Breakfasts--Juvenile literature. | Cooking--Juvenile literature. | LCGFT: Cookbooks.
Classification: LCC TX733 .V44 2017 (print) | LCC TX733 (ebook) | DDC 641.5/2--dc23

LC record available at https://lccn.loc.gov/2016019124

Manufactured in the United States of America
1-41346-23290-8/26/2016

Photo Acknowledgments
The images in this book are used with the permission of: © Alina Solovyova-Vincent/iStockphoto, p. 4; © Mighty Media, Inc., pp. 5 (top left), 5 (top right), 5 (bottom), 9 (top), 9 (bottom), 10, 11 (top), 11 (middle), 11 (bottom), 12, 13 (top), 13 (middle), 13 (bottom), 14, 15 (top), 15 (middle), 15 (bottom), 16, 17 (top), 17 (middle), 17 (bottom), 18, 19 (top), 19 (middle), 19 (bottom), 20, 21 (top), 21 (middle), 21 (bottom), 22, 23 (top), 23 (middle), 23 (bottom), 24, 25 (top), 25 (middle), 25 (bottom), 27 (top), 27 (middle), 27 (bottom), 28, 29 (top), 29 (middle), 29 (bottom); © Elena Elisseeva/Shutterstock Images, p. 6; © BravissimoS/Shutterstock Images, p. 7; © Pressmaster/Shutterstock Images, p. 8; © Alena Ozerova/Shutterstock Images, p. 30.

Front Cover: © Mighty Media, Inc.

CONTENTS

GROSS MORNING MEALS

Do you dream of starting your day with an oozing bowl of brains for breakfast? Have you ever wished for a side of slimy eyeballs alongside your cereal and toast? Revolting recipes may seem supergross. But they can actually be totally tasty!

Many people delight in being frightened by food. It is fun to make, serve, and eat foods that have nauseating names or look disgusting. But the key to these dishes is that they are actually delicious. Your friends and family will love gulping down chunky snot smoothies, blood-and-guts pastries, and other horrifying breakfasts!

Before You
GET STARTED

Cook Safely! Creating horrifying breakfasts means using many different kitchen tools and appliances. These items can be very hot or sharp. Make sure to get an adult's help whenever making a recipe that requires use of an oven, stove, or knife.

Be a Smart Chef! Cooking gross breakfasts can be messy. Ask an adult for permission before starting a new cooking project. Then make sure you have a clean workspace. Wash your hands often while cooking. If you have long hair, be sure to tie it back. Make sure your guests don't have any food allergies before cooking. Adjust the recipes if you need to. Make sure your stomach-churning breakfasts are safe to eat!

Tools You'll Need

Cooking can involve special tools and appliances. You will need the following items for these disgusting recipes:

- blender
- oven
- refrigerator
- stove or hot plate

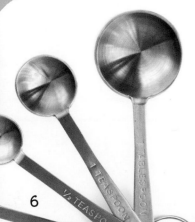

METRIC CONVERSION CHART

Use this handy chart to convert recipes to the metric system. If you can't find the conversion you need, ask an adult to help you find an online calculator!

STANDARD	METRIC
¼ teaspoon	1.2 milliliters
½ teaspoon	2.5 ml
¾ teaspoon	3.7 ml
1 teaspoon	5 ml
2 teaspoons	10 ml
1 tablespoon	15 ml
¼ cup	59 ml
⅓ cup	79 ml
½ cup	118 ml
⅔ cup	158 ml
¾ cup	177 ml
1 cup	237 ml

150 degrees Fahrenheit	66 degrees Celsius
300°F	149°C
350°F	177°C
400°F	204°C

1 ounce	28 grams
1 fluid ounce	30 milliliters
1 inch	2.5 centimeters
1 pound	0.5 kilograms

TURNING BREAKFAST TERRIFYING

Frightful Titles

When it comes to creating horrifying meals, a good title is a very important ingredient! An egg turns into a slimy eyeball, and oatmeal starts to look a lot like brains! Once everyday foods are named something sick, it becomes tough for diners to picture them as anything else. Be sure to tell friends and family what each dish is called before serving it. The disgusted faces they make are part of the fun!

Shocking Setups

In addition to disgusting titles, the way you present your revolting breakfast recipes is important. Fun, gross, or scary props will play up the horror of each dish. Picture fake insects swarming on the table. Serve your meals with toilet-paper napkins. Any small touch you can think of to grossify your table will add to the fun! Don't forget to **sanitize** your props before they touch the food. And make sure any props that are not **edible** are removed before your guests dig in! Keep things fun and delicious without putting your diners in danger.

SNOT SMOOTHIE

Whip up a quick and healthful mucus shake for breakfast. Those extra-thick globs of nose juice wash right down!

Ingredients

2 ripe bananas
½ cup milk
½ cup vanilla yogurt
1 cup cut-up or canned fruit, such as peaches, pears, or melons
½ cup sunflower or pumpkin seeds
1 handful spinach leaves
½ avocado
½ cup ice cubes

Tools

- knife
- cutting board
- blender
- measuring cups

Serves: 1–2
Preparation Time: 30 minutes

1. Peel and cut up the bananas, and put them in the blender.

2. Add the milk and yogurt to the blender.

3. Add the fruit, seeds, spinach, and avocado to the blender.

4. With an adult's help, turn on the blender and pulse 7 to 10 times, or until the ingredients are blended.

5. Add the ice cubes, and pulse some more. Stop when the mixture is smooth and creamy. No tissues needed for this delicious drink.

No dairy, no problem! Substitute almond milk, rice milk, or soy milk for dairy milk.

BOWL OF BRAINS

Become extra smart by eating brains for breakfast.
Don't worry about lumps in this nutritious dish.

Ingredients

¼ cup milk, plus a few extra
    splashes for serving
2 cups rolled oats
1 15-ounce can pumpkin puree
1 teaspoon vanilla extract
2 teaspoons pumpkin pie spice
2 tablespoons maple syrup, plus
    more for serving
¼ teaspoon salt
1 apple
¼ cup almonds
½ cup raspberry jam

Tools

• saucepan
• measuring cups
• measuring spoons
• mixing spoon
• peeler
• knife
• cutting board
• serving bowls
• small bowl

Serves: 4
Preparation Time: 10–30 minutes

1 In a saucepan over high heat, bring 3¾ cups water to a **boil** with an adult's help. Add ¼ cup milk and the oats. Then reduce the temperature to medium. Cook for 1 to 2 minutes.

2 Add the pumpkin puree, vanilla extract, pumpkin pie spice, 2 tablespoons maple syrup, and salt to the saucepan. Stir together.

2

3 Peel and chop the apple. Add it to the saucepan and stir. Cook for 3 to 10 minutes, or until the oats are cooked. Remove the saucepan from the heat.

 4 Chop the almonds into small pieces.

5 Scoop the oatmeal into bowls, and **garnish** each one with nuts, a splash of milk, and a bit of maple syrup.

3

6 Put the raspberry jam in a small bowl. Add 1 or 2 tablespoons of water, and stir until runny. Drizzle the jam over the brains for a bloody garnish. Then watch your guests grimace as they dig into these appetizing brains.

5

TIP

Make your own pumpkin pie spice. Just mix together 2 teaspoons ground cinnamon and ¼ teaspoon each of ground ginger, nutmeg, allspice, and ground cloves.

BLOODY EYEBALL EGGS

These slimy fried eyes will stare back at hungry diners!

Ingredients

2 sausage links
1 tablespoon butter
4 eggs
¼ cup ketchup

Tools

- measuring cups
- frying pan
- spatula
- knife
- cutting board
- serving plates
- table knife

Serves: 2–4
Preparation Time: 30 minutes

1. Put ¼ cup water and the sausages in the frying pan. With an adult's help, cook the sausages for 6 to 8 minutes over medium-high heat. Turn the sausages, and cook for 6 to 8 more minutes or until done. Remove the sausages, and let them cool.

2. Cut the tips off each sausage. Each tip should be about ¼ inch long.

3. Place the butter in the frying pan, and melt it over medium heat. Then crack an egg and drop it near the edge of the pan. Repeat with another egg.

4. Cook both eggs for 5 minutes, or until the whites are cooked through and the yolks are soft.

5. Remove each egg with a spatula and put it on a plate. Repeat steps 3 through 5 until the other eggs are cooked.

6. Use a table knife to decorate your eyeballs with ketchup veins. Then place a sausage tip in the middle of each egg for the pupil. Cut up the rest of the sausages to serve on the side. Your guests will gobble up these bloody eyeballs!

TIP

For a vegetarian breakfast, use two black olives for pupils instead of the sausage tips.

15

GREEN ZOMBIE FLESH AND OOZE

French toast becomes flaky zombie skin in this deadly dish! Don't forget the creamy zombie pus for dipping.

Ingredients

Ooze
3 ripe bananas
1 tablespoon maple syrup
1 teaspoon vanilla extract
1 teaspoon cinnamon
2 handfuls fresh baby spinach leaves
1½ cups milk

4 large slices of bread
2 tablespoons butter

Tools

- measuring spoons
- measuring cups
- blender
- large bowl
- frying pan
- spatula

Serves: 4
Preparation Time: 30–45 minutes

Peel the bananas. With an adult's help, blend the bananas, maple syrup, vanilla, cinnamon, spinach, and milk in the blender until mixed. This is your ooze. Measure out ¾ cup of the ooze, and put it in the refrigerator. Pour the rest into a large bowl.

 Soak each piece of bread in the bowl of ooze.

3 Melt the butter in the frying pan over medium heat.

4 Add the ooze-soaked slices of bread to the frying pan. Then cook for 3 to 4 minutes. Using a spatula, turn each slice over, and cook another 2 to 3 minutes. Add a spoonful of ooze to each, and cook for 1 to 2 more minutes.

5 Serve each scabby slice of fleshy toast with a heaping side of zombie ooze!

1

2

4

CRUSHED BONES

Bloody jam makes these broken bones an extra-sweet breakfast treat!

Ingredients

1 8-count package refrigerated
    cinnamon rolls
½ cup raspberry or
    strawberry jam

Tools

• knife
• cutting board
• baking sheet
• parchment paper
• oven mitts
• measuring cup
• measuring spoons
• serving plate

Serves: 4–6
Preparation Time: 30 minutes

1. **Preheat** the oven according to the cinnamon roll package. Separate the rolls into sections and unroll them. Cut each section in half.

1

2. Cover a baking sheet with parchment paper. Sculpt each roll section to look like a bone. Place the bones on the baking sheet.

3. Bake the bones for 10 to 12 minutes, or according to the package instructions. With an adult's help, take the baking sheet out of the oven, and let the bones cool.

2

4. Now break the bones. Split them into pieces of various sizes, and add 1 teaspoon of jam to each jagged bone end.

5. Bake the bones another 2 to 3 minutes.

6. Remove the baking sheet from the oven, and put the bones on a serving plate. Drench them in drippy jam blood. Then let diners dig through the wreckage to choose their bones!

TIP

To make your bones extra realistic, ask an adult help you look up bone images online. Shape your bones to look like the ones in the images.

4

SPIDER EGGS

The spooky spiderwebs in these **savory** hard-boiled eggs make for a creepy-crawly treat!

Ingredients

1 dozen eggs
1 teaspoon salt
¼ onion
2 teabags black tea
4 tablespoons soy sauce
1 2-inch piece peeled, fresh ginger

Tools

• large stockpot
• measuring spoons
• slotted spoon
• large bowl
• knife
• cutting board

Serves: 3–4
Preparation Time: 2½–3 hours

1. Place the eggs in the stockpot, and cover with cold water. Add the salt. With an adult's help, bring the water to a boil over high heat. Turn the temperature down to medium-low, and **simmer** for 15 minutes.

1

2. Carefully remove the pot from the heat. Using a slotted spoon, move the eggs to a large bowl, and fill with cool water. Let the eggs cool for 15 to 30 minutes. Ask an adult to help you drain the stockpot.

3. Gently crack each cooled egg on a countertop or table. Crack in several places on each egg. But don't remove the shells from the eggs.

3

4. Put the eggs back in the stockpot and cover them with water again. Chop the onion into small pieces. Add the teabags, soy sauce, ginger, and onion to the stockpot. Bring to a boil over high heat. Turn the temperature down to medium-low, and let the eggs simmer for 1 hour.

5. Carefully remove the pot from the heat and let the eggs cool in the liquid. Peel each egg when cool. Now startle squeamish diners with these web-covered eggs!

4

CLOGGED-DRAIN HAIR CLUMP CEREAL

These cereal stacks look just like matted clumps of hair you might fish out of a clogged drain!

Ingredients

2 tablespoons butter
3 tablespoons honey
1 cup chocolate chips
1 teaspoon vanilla extract
¼ teaspoon salt
3 large shredded wheat bundles
milk, for serving

Tools

- medium saucepan
- measuring spoons
- measuring cups
- mixing spoon
- baking sheet
- waxed paper
- serving bowl

Serves: 4–6
**Preparation Time: 1 hour
(15–30 minutes active)**

1

 Melt the butter in a saucepan over medium heat. Add the honey, chocolate chips, vanilla, and salt. Stir until the chocolate is melted and the ingredients are combined and smooth. Remove the pan from heat.

 Loosen and break up the wheat bundles with clean hands. Then place the bundles in the saucepan with the chocolate mixture. Gently stir until all the shredded wheat is coated with chocolate.

2

 Line a baking sheet with waxed paper.

4 Scoop similar-sized clumps of the chocolate-coated wheat onto the waxed paper. Let them cool in the refrigerator for 30 to 45 minutes.

4

 Your clumps are ready to serve! A swig of milk helps hungry diners wash these hairy tangles down their drains!

BLOOD AND GUTS

A terrifying treat for gore-loving guests.

Ingredients

Filling

¾ cup brown sugar

½ cup granulated sugar

1 tablespoon cinnamon

1 tablespoon vanilla extract

½ teaspoon salt

2 tablespoons butter

Dough

2½ cups all-purpose flour, plus more
    for rolling out dough

⅓ cup granulated sugar

1½ teaspoons baking powder

½ teaspoon baking soda

½ teaspoon salt

1 cup buttermilk

4 tablespoons butter, melted

cooking spray

Frosting

4 ounces cream cheese, softened

1 cup powdered sugar

4 tablespoons buttermilk

Sauce

⅔ cup raspberry jam

¼ cup light corn syrup

½ teaspoon liquid red food coloring

Tools

• measuring cups

• measuring spoons

• mixing bowls of various sizes

• mixing spoons

• **whisk**

• rolling pin

• knife

• cutting board

• 9 x 13-inch baking dish

• oven mitts

• fork

• table knife

Serves: 4–6

Preparation Time: 30–45 minutes

1. Preheat the oven to 425°F. Mix the filling ingredients together in a medium bowl, and set it aside.

1

2. Next, make the dough. In a large bowl, stir together the flour, granulated sugar, baking powder, baking soda, and salt. In a small bowl, whisk the buttermilk and melted butter together. Mix gently with the dry ingredients. Stop as soon as the ingredients are combined. **Knead** the dough for 1 or 2 minutes. Then divide it into two equal chunks.

3. Sprinkle flour over a clean work surface. Then roll one chunk of dough into a rectangle. It should be a little bigger than a piece of notebook paper. Spread one-half of the filling evenly across dough, leaving space around the edges. Then roll the dough up and pinch the ends. Repeat with the other chunk of dough and the rest of the filling.

3

4. Coat the baking dish with cooking spray. Cut the dough into pieces of many different sizes. These will be your cinnamon rolls. Place the pieces in the baking dish. Scoop 2 tablespoons of jam on top. With an adult's help, bake for 15 to 18 minutes, and remove from oven.

5. Now make the frosting. Put the cream cheese and powdered sugar in a bowl. Blend them with a fork. Add the buttermilk, 1 tablespoon at a time. Spread the frosting on top of the baked rolls.

4

6. Finally, make the sauce. In a small bowl, stir together the rest of the jam, corn syrup, and food coloring. Drizzle the sauce over the warm rolls. These monster guts may look horrifying, but they will taste delicious!

SPOOKY SKULL EGGS

A grinning skeleton egg with a yummy yolk filling makes a tasty treat for breakfast, brunch, or anytime!

Ingredients

1 dozen eggs
1¼ teaspoon salt
½ cup mayonnaise
1 tablespoon mustard
¼ teaspoon pepper
2 teaspoons Worcestershire sauce
1 **dash** hot sauce
paprika
ketchup, for serving

Tools

- large stockpot
- measuring spoons
- slotted spoon
- mixing bowls, various sizes
- knife
- cutting board
- spoon
- fork
- measuring cups
- drinking straws
- coffee stir straws

Serves: 4–5
Preparation Time: 1 hour

Place the eggs in the stockpot and cover with cold water. Add 1 teaspoon salt. With an adult's help, bring to a boil over high heat. Turn the temperature down to medium-low, and simmer for 15 minutes.

Carefully remove the pot from heat. Using a slotted spoon, move the eggs to a large bowl, and fill it with cool water. Let the eggs cool for 15 to 30 minutes.

Crack the eggs and carefully peel them.

4 With an adult's help, slice each egg in half lengthwise, and remove the yolks with a spoon. Put the yolks in a bowl.

5 Mash the yolks together using the back of a fork. Mix in the mayonnaise, mustard, ¼ teaspoon salt, pepper, Worcestershire sauce, and hot sauce. This makes a filling.

Skull Eggs continued next page

3

4

5

Have an adult help you look up pictures of skulls online to make sure yours look realistic.

Skull Eggs, continued

6

6 Scoop 1 tablespoon of filling into each egg white. Sprinkle each egg with paprika. Pair up each egg half with another egg half, so the two halves stick together. The filling should seal them. These are your skulls.

7 Using a drinking straw, poke two holes in each egg for eyes.

8 Using the same straw, carefully poke a hole for the nose.

9 Poke small holes using the coffee stir straw to make rows of teeth in each skull.

10 Arrange the skulls on a plate. Drizzle ketchup over them for some extra flare, and dish up your grinning skulls at your next brunch.

7

9

WRAPPING UP

Cleaning Up

Once you are done cooking, it is time to clean up! Make sure to wipe up spills, wash dishes, and clear the table. Wash and put away any props you used that don't belong in the kitchen. Make sure any leftovers are properly packaged and refrigerated.

Keep Cooking!

Get inspired by your disgusting breakfast dishes. Think up ways to cook up new versions of the revolting recipes you tried. Or create your own! Think gross, and keep on cooking!

GLOSSARY

boil: liquid that has become so hot that bubbles form and rise to the top

dash: a very small amount

edible: something that can be safely eaten

garnish: to decorate food before serving it

knead: to work, press, and fold dough with one's hands until it is smooth

preheat: to heat an oven to the required temperature before putting in the food

sanitize: to clean something so it is free of germs

savory: smelling and tasting good

simmer: to cook something in water that is not quite boiling and has very small bubbles

vegetarian: without meat

whisk: to stir very quickly using a fork or a tool made of curved wire, also called a whisk

FURTHER INFORMATION

Cooking with Kids
http://www.foodnetwork.com/recipes/
packages/recipes-for-kids/cooking-with-kids/
recipes-kids-can-make.html
Learn tips and tricks to get you started in the
kitchen.

**Cornell, Kari A. *Slurpable Smoothies
and Drinks.*** Minneapolis: Millbrook Press, 2014.
Learn how to blend up some mouthwatering
beverages for some tasty breakfast treats.

Halloween Breakfast
http://www.mrbreakfast.com/halloween.asp
Check out even more spooky breakfast recipes
perfect for startling your family and friends.

**Taste of Home. *Taste of Home Kid
Approved Cookbook.*** Greendale, WI: Taste
of Home Books, 2012.
These kid-approved recipes will get you cooking
in no time.

INDEX